SURVIVING

"THE PIED PIPER"

THE UNTOLD STORY

LIFE BEFORE AND AFTER THE TRIAL

LISA VANALLEN

Published by Pelican Gang Ent.
No part of this publication may be reproduced, stored in a retrieval
system, or transmitted in any form or by any means, electronic,
mechanical, photocopying, recording, scanning, or otherwise, except as
permitted under Section 107 or 108 of the 1976 United States Copyright
Act, without the prior permission of the Publisher and author.
SURVIVING "THE PIED PIPER"/LISA VANALLEN

ISBN-13: 978-1-7337156-0-7

ISBN-10: 1-7337156-0-6

DEDICATION

To my children:

The love I have for all of you is unconditional. You have given me strength I didn't know I had, love I have always been searching for and happiness I never knew existed. I'd like to thank God for blessing me with all of you.

FOREWORD

I fell in love the first time I saw you.
*One touch. One look. I knew you were the one and you would
be mine.*

I came along to break the spell.
*You filled an empty space in my life, and I strived to fill the
voids in your heart where a longing for love once dwelled.*

I've watched you grow despite heartache, trauma and pain.
*I pledge to join with you in your fight to bring awareness and
helping others to heal and be whole again.*

No more tears!
Together we'll face whatever comes our way.

—Your Loving Fiancé

PROLOGUE

The means to survive is often not something we naturally have but situations in life force us to adapt in order to make it through to the other side. I guess I can say I started to develop them when I was young.

I was born in Hartford, Connecticut (June 11, 1980) to parents too young to have me and not equipped enough to handle the role. I ended up in foster care on Capen Street at the tender age of 1 right along with my newborn-brother.

I don't remember much from my first couple of years there, but I know I must have missed my mom. I never stopped looking for her to come get me while I was there, even up until the day I was adopted.

Ms. Wilburn was the person in charge at the time. She had no use for me. In my eyes she could never be my mother or take her place. She knew it too and resented me for it. When it came to my brother, she was nice and treated him as her own, because he was a newborn baby. I was one of the younger kids there (aside from my brother) and the only girl in a house full of boys. However, she made no allowances for me. At 3-years-old, I ran with the boys and dressed like them too, as she only put me in the clothes that were there. She didn't buy any girl clothes. She almost never did my hair. As long as I got to go outside, I didn't care. We'd play in the graveyard behind the house and make mud pies. Those were the carefree times where I could forget the day to day strife of being in that place.

Ms. Wilburn was a very strict woman with a mean spirit even though she went to church very often. (We spent all the holidays there!) We would have to eat whatever she cooked. Now, I know you might be saying, "well that's nothing", but to a kid it's a pretty big deal. Parents will often attempt to make the foods their children will eat and sometimes express their love for them by making the foods they love. It was clear that although Ms. Wilburn wanted to be seen as a parental figure, a lot of her actions were cold and devoid of love. It's one thing if it's due to being impoverished, but another if they just don't care enough to consider doing so. Fish with bones in it, is something I do not eat still to this very day. As a kid I was made to eat it, but at 3-years-old, you don't know how to take out the bones beforehand. I would choke on them, but she didn't seem to be concerned. If you were still hungry after dinner, then that was your problem. She never gave any extra snack or helpings to fill you up. There were plenty of times we'd go to bed hungry even after having dinner. It became so unbearable after a while that one night, I snuck into the kitchen. I can remember the roaches scattering as I turned on the light. I stacked some things on top of each other in order to reach the cabinet to grab the peanut butter and eat it from the jar. This, I would do for several nights. However, one night she got suspicious that someone was sneaking in the kitchen to get the peanut butter. I don't know if I left a mess or left something out of place, but she knew.

I'll never forget the look on her face that night as she made us get up and out of beds to line up one-by-one. I could feel the anxiety taking over me as we were made to open our mouths, so she could check our breath for peanut butter. I was scared and trying not to break before she got to me. I wanted to be anywhere but there. Finally, it's my turn for inspection. I remember my heart beating fast as I could already anticipate the beating she later gave me.

That wasn't the worse trauma I faced there. Being the only girl amongst all boys that are not siblings with little to no supervision is usually a recipe for disaster, especially with older children in the mix.

Some of the older teenage boys used to have friends come over to play basketball. These friends would be the ones to take away my innocence. They would watch me as I went to the bathroom and often barged in, because the latch on the door was not a secure one. Even worse, they'd often corner me when I was alone and take turns making me jack them off. I knew it felt disgusting and wrong deep down inside, but I didn't know any better. I was also afraid to piss them off and afraid of what would happen if I told. Besides, who would I tell? Who was in my corner? No one taught me about "good touch or bad touch". I was 4-years old, alone and unprotected, which makes for easy prey for those with a predatory mind.

As I got older (5 or 6), I would have some moments where I would get away from Ms. Wilburn and foster care. My grandma would come get me sometimes and take me to McDonald's. Sometimes, my aunt would come to get me and take me to spend the night at her house. At the end of it all, I still ended up right back at foster care which put a damper on the time period before I'd return. I often cried not to go back and lucky for me, it finally resonated. Not with blood relatives, but still very much family. My grandmother's friend would often come to visit me when my grandmother was too busy. My grandmother used to tell her about me all the time, so she decided to come see me when my grandmother was not able. This is how we developed our own special bond. I was even invited to be in her wedding.

She would be the one to adopt me. That was one of the happiest days of my life. I left that place and did not look back. It only hit me later, that I had really left my brother behind. I knew he would be okay because she (Ms. Wilburn) could pass herself off as a mother to him being that he came to foster care young and didn't know any better. All I knew is that I had made it out of there, but not without damage. The trauma I experienced in that place would have me do things like repeatedly turn the stack of magazines over that my new mom had in the bathroom because I felt that the people on the cover were watching me. I may have left that place, but certain elements or experiences didn't leave me.

The ordeal of being thrusted into the foster care system so young, having no stable family beginnings, and the sexual abuse would cause me to have an emptiness or void within myself. These voids, people will always find themselves trying to fill and often with the wrong people in the wrong places. It is those same voids and issues of abandonment that made me vulnerable to those with predatory, abusive, or sociopathic type characteristics. The sexual abuse that I experienced at an early age gave me an early perception that sex was mostly for someone else's pleasure. The manifestation would play out in a lot of my relationships as I forgot about loving and pleasing the most important person, which is myself.

(Photo at 1-years-old)

The old proverb teaches that death and life are in the power of the tongue. What we speak on, we give life and power to. So as to not give any more power to one of many sexual predators, this work is intentional in using their name as less as possible. Power to all survivors! May you no longer be oppressed by the silence, lack of support and the trauma.

Chapter 1

Today's the day! Today is the day that I speak a truth I've been speaking for well over a decade. Now is the time they are ready to listen.

As I sit here in this styling chair waiting for the makeup artist and stylist to prep me, I turned to face the mirror beside me. No make-up. No slayed coif. Just me! Raw, bare-faced, and vulnerable. I can honestly say with confidence at this stage in my life, I am quite comfortable and love the image I see reflected back at me. I contribute it all to the love I grew to have for "just me".

It wasn't always this way. I had to grow after going through a lot of things to become this person. They say in order to really move forward a person must really go backwards.

I'd have to take it all the way back to 1998, a pivotal moment in my young, adolescent life when I met the future self-proclaimed "Pied Piper" of R&B. It was a nickname he would give himself a decade later, but what I nor the world realized, was just how true to form the title would be.

It all started out with me helping out a friend. A longtime male friend of mine wanted me to accompany his girlfriend, an aspiring singer, to a video shoot as an extra because he didn't want her to go alone. I was 17, and ready for my close up, plus I didn't think twice about what type of environment that comes with artists and the music industry. I was going to support my friend's girlfriend and hoped to see my face flash across the screen for half a second at least, just so that I could show all my friends that I was there, that's all. "That's me with the blonde bob and cute outfit!" is what I anticipated on saying.

The video shoot was taking place at a mansion in Alpharetta, Georgia in the evening. We were told to bring a change of clothes that would fit the various scenes they were shooting. The meeting point to get to the shoot was actually a church so no one would know the exact location. A shuttle came to pick everyone up and take them to the mansion. Once we got there, we had to sign in and were told where to go afterwards to get ready to shoot different scenes from the video.

During the downtime of shooting scenes for the video, a guy came up to me, whom I later found out was a cousin. He told me that, Rob wanted to talk to me. In my mind, I'm wondering who Rob could be, so I asked him. When he answered with "R Kelly", it threw me off a bit as I was only 17 and probably one of the youngest females at the shoot. I paused for a minute, because I was trying to figure out what he could possibly want with me. Did I do something wrong? Did he want to kick me off the set? I didn't know what to think. I definitely was not expecting the exchange that happened next.

I followed the guy to another part of the mansion nervously, and a bit puzzled. When I reached the area where he was sitting, after we exchanged pleasantries he began to ask me questions. Not normal questions that one would ask someone they just met and especially not a young girl you just met. He asked if I had a boyfriend. I told him I didn't. He asked my age and I told him I was 17. Next, he asked if my mom would let me come to Chicago to which I replied that she would, even though I had not asked her at all. In my mind I thought that was the answer he would have liked to hear, and I didn't want to say no to someone of his caliber. He continued to ask more questions about me and my life. He was very deliberate in his questioning for a reason. He needed to gauge if I presented him with a situation that he could easily maneuver and manipulate or if there would be too many obstacles, like overprotective parents or a boyfriend. I just thought he was trying to get to know me. What should have been red flags, to me, felt like someone taking an interest in me. It made me feel special and this is something I haven't yet experienced to this degree, especially from the opposite sex.

I started to shiver a little as the breeze picked up. He seemed to be concerned asked me if I was cold. I told him that I was, so he asked if I wanted to go sit on the tour bus. Looking back this definitely should have been another red flag given the differences in our ages and he was basically a stranger, even though he was a celebrity. However, at the time, I was happy to talk with him and the fact that he seemed to have an interest in getting to know me made me feel a bit at ease. Once we got on the tour bus, we talked some more.

All of a sudden, he started kissing me. Then kissing led to touching. Touching, then led to him pushing me back onto the bed in the tour bus and us having sex. That's not what I came there for, but I was now in a situation where I didn't know or think to be mindful. I didn't want to have sex, but I also didn't want to disappoint him by telling him to stop. Besides, he did take an interest in me out of all the girls there. This is what I told myself, at least. I do realize now that I wasn't in the best of headspace to make the best decisions given my background and upbringing. At the time he seemed to fill a void within me, but in reality, he'd be the one to create more and exploit the ones that already existed.

When it was over, he told me I can remain there on the bus to rest and take shelter from the cold. He got off the bus to go shoot some more of the video. In between scenes, he would come back to the bus, but he insisted that I continue to stay on the bus. I thought he just wanted me to stay on, so we could talk, but looking back it's more likely that he didn't want anyone to see me get off the bus. I remained on the bus until the video shoot wrapped, which wasn't until the next morning. We exchanged numbers and he told me to call him.

It was a whole month before I gathered up the nerve to call, because I really didn't know what to say. Even though, we had sex on the tour bus the month prior, I still was not at ease enough to carry on a full conversation with a grown man. I finally got the nerve to dial the number and he picked up. There wasn't much of a conversation to be honest. After I identified myself, he immediately asked when I would be able to get to Chicago.

After I gave him a date, he put me in contact with his assistant, June Brown. He had instructed me on what to do. He sent me the money to get the stuff I needed. I didn't have a State ID at the time, but I had to get one to get a plane ticket. Once I got to Chicago, he said he would have a driver waiting to pick me up from the airport. Since I paid for everything with the money he gave me, there was really no paper trail for him.

The permission from my mother was what I needed next. I asked at the most convenient time for me but the most inconvenient time for my mom. She was carrying the weight of the world on her shoulders at that moment. Her mom had just had a stroke and the doctors also diagnosed her with cancer. My mom was the one taking care of her on top of everything else she was doing. I don't think she had the strength to fight me on it, so she gave in, but she wanted a number where she could contact me. It was an unfair advantage that worked in my favor. I did give her the number to the studio, so she could check on me from time to time, so she would be somewhat at ease.

Typically, a young teen traveling alone on a trip to Chicago under these conditions, sounds like a recipe for disaster. I was a bit headstrong and thought that I would be able to handle whatever came my way.

You see, a year earlier, at 16, I was a little rebellious and at the time, I was not getting along well with my mom (normal teenage stuff). I thought it would be a great idea if I went to stay with my favorite cousin for a while in Minneapolis, Minnesota. It would give me some time to bond with members of my birth mom's side of the family. In my mind, I would be having the time of my life soon. Little did I know that this trip will be a test of my will and a testament to the lengths I would go to make a situation work even if it wasn't conducive to me personally. Some things we do subconsciously but are unaware of until we take the time to really examine them.

Soon as I got there, I was hit with a stark reality. My aunt, although a mother, was not the same as my mother and not your typical mother. Her style of "parenting" was the survival of the fittest approach. She didn't cook much or buy groceries, so we had to figure out a way to eat. She also didn't give us a key, so if you got home when she wasn't there, you couldn't get in. I was often stuck outside in the midst of a blizzard. I had to adapt fast. I started to ride the bus for hours on end and stay on until the route ended to keep warm and because I had nowhere else to go at the time. If friends were at home, I'd stay with them until she came back, and I could get into the house. Sometimes that wouldn't be until the next morning.

I had very little money. On top of having to feed myself, I needed clothes, hygiene products, plus books and supplies for the school I was attending downtown. I had enrolled in an alternative school since all the regular schools were filled to capacity. I developed my hustling spirit in this way because I was determined to figure out how to survive this situation so that I wouldn't have to go back home and admit defeat. I would flip candy for profit or get things at a discount at the mall and other places then resell them in order to get the money for the things that I needed. I even taught myself how to braid hair, so I could become a stylist to other girls that I knew. I would continue to do this until one of my other aunts caught wind of how I was living and decided to send me back home.

My adaptability and survivor's mentality I further developed during my 6-month stint in Minneapolis had my 17-year-old self, confident that I would be fine on this trip to Chicago. I also thought I would eventually have his love and affection to protect and help guide me.

Chapter 2

On the way to Chicago, I was overwhelmed with emotions. I was excited because this was my first big trip and nervous because I was going to see him again. I was wondering what I would say when I first saw him or what he would say to me. Our conversation before I embarked on this journey was very short. I didn't know exactly what I was about to walk into, but overall, my thoughts were positive.

When I landed, I was greeted by a driver that held a sign with my name on it, which made me feel like someone of importance. First, I was taken to a hotel so that I could drop off my bags and then the driver took me to the studio. The studio, Chicago Trax, was kind of close to the hood. Cabrini Green housing projects was not far from it, so there was a big fence around it to keep people from easily accessing the studio. It was at least 15 feet tall. I had to push the call button, in order for someone to let me inside. After identifying myself and whom I was there to see for the person who answered the page, there was an awkward silence as they went to confirm if I was supposed to be there. I was finally let inside the gate and one of his runners had come to meet me at the door.

There were plenty of rooms inside the studio, I noticed, as we walked through the building. I finally, reached the studio where he was doing his recording for the day. Once inside, we greeted each other and exchanged hugs. That day, we just chilled and listened to some music. I was glad I made it there safely and his interest seemed to still be there.

What was clear to me from the first couple of days of being there was that he definitely had a set routine that he kept. He was very methodical in that way. He would definitely spend time in the studio until the wee hours of the morning before going to sleep. However, his days didn't really start until the evening because of not getting to sleep until it's almost time for the sun to rise. After getting up, he'd go eat. Then, he would go record in the studio for some time. After that, we'd hop in his Range Rover or Lincoln Navigator to go to Hoops, which was a 24-hour gym. Around this time, it would be close to midnight and we'd stay for an hour or two. We'd hit Rock 'n' Roll McDonalds downtown for something to eat before finally finishing the night off with more studio time. It was his favorite place to get a grilled chicken sandwich with lettuce, tomato and no bread plus a coffee to drink. Sometimes we'd go eat at Portillo's during the day where he'd get a hot dog with mayo, lettuce and tomato.

Afterwards, I'd usually be in the studio with him lying on the couch or off watching movies in another room.

Sometimes it did get boring in a way because it was very repetitive. However, being in the studio with him creating music made up for it. He had a way with words and melodies that captivated you, which he definitely knew and would use to his advantage.

I was only supposed to stay briefly, as I had not one, but two jobs waiting for me back at home. I worked in retail at two neighboring department stores in the mall part-time. My intentions were to stay only for the weekend, but he kept intentionally making me miss my flight. Even though it frustrated me a little, it felt good to have someone to make you feel needed and wanted in that kind of way.

When I did finally make it back home, he kept calling for me to come back. I traveled back up there about a week later. This time, however, he didn't want me to go back home at all. I was thinking that he cared about me that much and just always wanted me around. It was actually the first step of him gaining more control in the relationship.

I told him that I would eventually be fired from my job if I keep missing my flight to go back home since I had been missing work. So, he asked me about how much I make in pay a week. I replied that I was making around $300 a week, which was a lot to a 17-year-old in '97. He responded by going into his pocket and pulling out $300 and handing it to me.

There were no more discussions about my job after that. There were also no discussions about me staying. I was just....there, and he knew it. From then, on, wherever he would be, so would I. From late nights in the studios and many hotels when he would travel for work and events. We were attached at the hip and for most part that goes beyond figuratively speaking. He was a sex nympho with an insatiable appetite. He'd want to have sex at least 3 times or more a day.

(Taken at the video shoot for "A Woman's Threat")

Chapter 3

Life with him started out fun, and I was having the time of my life. It was fine, until he got comfortable and convinced that I was not about to just go home at the spur of the moment and that I seemed content in the dependency on him. He gradually started to introduce me to different things, such as weird fetishes, and other people. He was slowly integrating the real person he was into our relationship, while testing how much of himself he was able to incorporate without me giving complete resistance.

He insisted on keeping mementoes of his moments of pleasure, so he liked to bring cameras around when he had sex. He would often record us having sex and liked for me to call him "Daddy". Sex with him had some mechanical elements to it, because he would coach you the whole time. He'd tell you where to put your hand, how to lay, when to poke your butt out, how to moan, etc. It's like, you're always on set at a porn shoot and he was the director. He liked it when you'd speak in a high-pitched voice, tell him about how you got your shape from your momma, or things of that manner. That was just the tip of the iceberg. What lie in wait underneath the surface was nothing I could have imagined.

He was a bit of an exhibitionist but in an oppressive kind of way. Sometimes he would be in the studio recording and just start jacking off, no matter who was in the room. The runners would come in and give him messages, other guys might be in the room, and the engineer was there, mostly. However, everyone pretended as if there was nothing going on and everything was normal. They didn't say anything. Maybe they chalked it up to one of those weird quirks that came along with working with an artist. Some artists brought drugs for inspiration, but he brought his penis. Either that, or they were just too afraid to say anything for fear of losing their jobs.

Before we took a trip to Los Angeles once, he made sure to give me a little "pep talk". By this time, it had become routine for him to give these talks when it came to things I may be uncomfortable with or things I didn't really want to do. He said he really wanted to have his first threesome. He went on and on about how he'd never done it before and that he would really like it if his first threesome could be with me.

I didn't really say much about it to him, but in my mind the thoughts were turning. I was thinking that I didn't want to do the threesome, because I didn't really want to share him with another person. However, I was also thinking that since he was a famous man expressing to me about a first-time experience that he wants to have with me, it may not be good to tell him no. He could just as easily go pick another female to do it with and I didn't want that. I should feel special that he picked me to have this new experience. It was completely the wrong thought path to have but I was 17 and I loved a man who took the time to make me feel like I was unique. I felt somewhat obligated to do it.

I did it to please him, but I got very little pleasure out of it. I was jealous because this girl had her hands on my man and he was touching her. Apart from that, she wouldn't stop performing. What I mean is that, she was obviously someone that was an aspiring singer looking to get put on in the industry. There was a moment, when he left the two of us alone in the hotel room together. This chick would not sit down. She was constantly singing or dancing or both as if she was auditioning, or to show that she had a one up on me because of her talent and that she should be the main girl. I don't know what her deal was, I just know that I was annoyed.

I hoped that this would be the end of it, now that he had fulfilled his fantasy, but it wasn't. He would ask again more frequently and with more aspiring wannabes in the lineup. He'd also have a camera rolling to record every minute. I later realized, that he had more than likely deceived me about his desired "first-time experience". It was something he was already into doing. He just needed to prime me to get me on board. He seemed to develop an insatiable appetite for threesomes over time.

I grew tired of them and was hoping he would do the same, but it only got more rampant. No one could really come around without him initiating one. Most times when he introduced me to another female, I could safely bet the house that a threesome would surely follow. It's something I shouldn't have allowed, but I loved him, and he made me feel as if he loved me too. He even mentioned to me at one point that, his mom told him that if a woman loved a man, she wouldn't try to change him. Although, I didn't fully believe that, I did love him and thought I could lowkey change him over time.

Some of the girls, I ended up being pretty cool with, oddly enough. There was one in particular, I was really cool with. We'd often joke amongst ourselves. One joke in particular, involved him and his hygiene or lack thereof. He didn't always like to bathe. He would often have sex right after playing basketball or have sex and just go about his day without hitting the shower first. He didn't change his socks much, so his feet stunk. I can't recall a time I saw him brush his teeth, however he would have a dentist come to clean them. He would also have his colon cleansed often. However, he would often have an odor that told it all.

Normally, people shower after sex, sweaty games of basketball or bowel movements, but that wasn't in his daily routine. He would hit the stage like that as well. It's crazy thinking about how he used to pump in the middle of the stage while all the females went wild over him. He'd probably had just come from having sex or playing ball. He would often wear no underwear but plenty of B.O. If they only knew.

The girl I was cool with and myself, started calling him Pepè Le Pew (the skunk from the Warner Brothers cartoons) due to some pegging sessions where we would penetrate him anally. That was one of his favorite things to do. He was still very much in control as he moved his hips back against whomever was doing the pegging. This is how we first came up with the name. So, in that moment and when he would take off his clothes, I would say to her, "Pepè Le Pew on you!", which meant the skunk smell is on you. She would start laughing and in turn he would start laughing, not realizing that we were talking about him. That would help provide some comic relief for me from the stress of the situation because I was always hesitant to engage in threesomes continuously. I had found comfort in a few coping mechanisms; this was one of them.

Sometimes, I would pretend that I was trying to be romantic, and I would run him some bath water. Deep down, I really did care about him despite how I felt about the threesomes and wanted him to do better. I could only do this at the hotels, because at the studio, they didn't have bathtubs, only showers.

I would try to be sexy and offer to wash him off in an attempt to really wash away the funk. I never wanted to offend him by telling him he stunk. He once told me a story about when he was younger that the girls didn't like him, and how he had a lot of pimples, which could possibly indicate he had problems with hygiene even then. It could have been something he just never really improved in as he grew older. It's sad, now that I think back on how I cared so much about his feelings even when he didn't seem to show a lot of care for mine.

He also had this huge obsession with my butt. He loved to rub on it, when we were together. It would later be the inspiration to one of the songs he wrote, "Feelin on Yo Booty". He liked to bury his face in my butt as he sung the words "Boooty!" and then he would burst out laughing. He told me that girls were buying bodies to look like mine, which would make me feel good as well as putting my name in his track "Birthday Song".

These feel-good moments were often overshadowed by feelings of somberness, shame, and an all-around dirtiness. This unclean feeling that I felt inside could only be suppressed by taking long bubble baths and I took them every chance I could get.

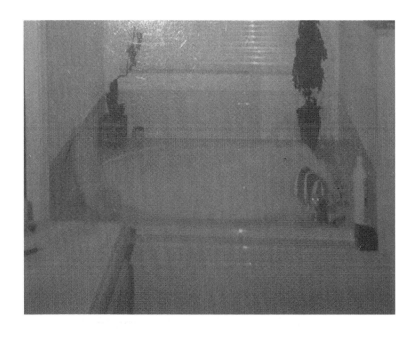

Chapter 4

There were things that he did that had me baffled, angry and/or confused, but my love for him and the need for him to love me kept me hanging on through most of it.

During the times I was in Chicago, my mom would often call, and she'd be frantic because she would have made many more calls before without my knowledge before she got through to me again. No one would tell me that she had called. This would have her in a state of panic because she wasn't able to speak to me for extended periods of time. I had to calm her down and assure her I was fine, when in reality I was not in the most ideal situation.

He also wouldn't allow me to consort with the staff and mainly other males and he would even forbid them to speak to me. It's a weird space to be in when you're cheerful speaking to everyone when you walk into a room but get nothing but deafening silence in return. Once, a male friend of his walked into the studio and started speaking to everyone. It was a natural response to speak back to him. This made him upset. He told me I wasn't to speak to anyone and that I needed to keep my eyes straight ahead. At first glance, it would make you appear like a stuck-up bitch that only had eyes for him. A deeper look revealed it for what it was. It was him, controlling the situation, myself and the people around him. It was also a way for him to control the outflow of information about him to others and a reminder that you were his property. I didn't want to make him upset, so I just did what he asked of me.

I recall, one of a few times during a threesome, I cried. I just really didn't want to do it. Instead of him consoling me, he asked what I was crying for then proceeded to basically tell me I was ruining his footage. He couldn't do anything with my tears. If I still refused, he often had sex without me, but with me on the other side of the bed with nowhere else to go. Another time I broke down, he yelled that it was "just sex". He had told me prior that he didn't connect any emotions to sex, which is why when it's over he would make everyone get dressed. There is no cuddling afterwards. He would have sex with other women but didn't trust them enough to sleep around them, so they would have to leave, or we would often leave and go home, where we slept in bed together.

If you had to pee, he didn't want to hear it. He wanted you to turn on the sink, so he wouldn't hear the sound of you peeing in the toilet. However, he didn't mind you hearing him pee and will attempt to carry on a full conversation with you while he was having a bowel movement. If that wasn't enough he'd often want me to squeeze in the stall with him to inhale his foul odor. He was a narcissist in that way that had a crazy obsession with control and often in demeaning way.

He once made a proposition to pee on me, adding he would "love to pee on my big ass" as if to convince me to agree. Needless to say, I was not with that at all. Having a threesome, is one thing and dealing with the body odor was another, but to outright piss on me would be outright degrading even though he didn't see it that way. I just uncomfortably laughed it off and he never brought it up again.

He had a way of figuring out where the boundaries were with people. He would push and push until he was met with resistance.

Although he had made me feel like I was his woman, I would find out things from the girls that I was cool with since I had all of their numbers. I would know who was coming into town before he did. Through them, I would also find out who else he was sleeping with.

He was the type of person that was really cheap with a lot of the other females he was dealing with. He didn't have any problems giving me money, but he knew that I was under the impression that we were in a relationship. I wasn't a gold digger nor was I trying to be famous through him. If I asked him for something, it was related to something that I actually needed more so than something I wanted.

Even then, he still had to insert control over the situation. If I wanted to go to the mall to get some things, he had to see what I was wearing. If it was form fitting, then I had to change. One time I ended up wearing his 2X shorts because I told him at the time that I didn't have anything to change into, which was kind of a lie because I just didn't feel like changing at the time. Since I was a size 2 at the time, I looked ridiculous walking around in the mall, but that was his way of ensuring you didn't really attract the attention of other men. He also didn't want me to talk to anyone there, but it's kind of hard to shop at times without saying something at least to the people that worked there.

He was really insistent on me not speaking to people in general, not just in the studio or out at the mall. Even, if it was his friends, which I found odd. Most men would want their friends to like their girl somewhat if they have to be around them in group settings. Not him, he'd want you to be the biggest bitch ever to them. Not speaking, sucking your teeth or rolling your eyes at them when they did speak is what he preferred. What did he really think of his friends if he insisted on this type of disrespect?

Towards the beginning of the relationship, I did speak to a friend of his and not only did he get upset, but he slapped me. I was very taken aback, because in my eyes, I didn't do anything wrong. In the midst of my crying, he told me that he loved me but that I just had to listen to "daddy" as if I were his child that he was protecting through discipline. He had a way of saying things, to make a young, naïve mind pliable, and moldable like putty in his hands. His intimidation factor and being the source of cash and other perks worked for the others around him.

He was very territorial with the girls in his camp, such as his dancers and with some of the artists. He had to always be the one pulling the strings. He had some working under and around him with a pay wage that intentionally made them dependent on him. While on tour, he was paying some of his artists only $25 a week in which they were to use this for food, hygiene, and transportation while on tour. This left a lot of them starving at times. Since, I had gotten close with some of the artists, I would look out for them by ordering room service in surplus. They became like brothers to me. This is how I got cool with one of the guys from the R&B

group, Talent, who would later hold a very private item for me. However, I knew to keep our interaction limited. I was at this time, very cognizant of the rules even though I bent them a little.

A second incident where I slipped up and spoke to someone in front of him, happened while we were on the tour bus. On the tour bus, we would often vibe and have a good time. It was often a party type atmosphere. I was having lots of fun, so I wasn't thinking about him not wanting me to speak to people. We were all laughing and having a lot of fun. One of his friends said something funny to me and quite naturally I laughed and replied back with something funny. He didn't find it funny at all. At this point, he grabbed me up out of my seat and took me towards the bathroom. I didn't even turn to look at the other people on the bus, I can only imagine their expressions or inner thoughts. I could only focus on where we were going and what was about to happen.

Once inside the bathroom, he started cursing me out. I'm looking at him visibly upset and I'm just in a frozen state. He then proceeded to spank me, like a daddy spanking his daughter as he continued to curse me out. He spanked me until I began to cry. It took for me to cry in order for him to stop. Some females often look for their dad in the men they date, but this is not the type of relation they are looking for at all. Afterwards, he came with the same spiel as he grabbed my face, about how he loved me. He said he was only trying to teach me that I should "listen to daddy". I didn't have a father growing up, but I didn't need nor want him to be that. I wouldn't do the things I did with him with my father.

He loved to be called "daddy" during sex, but I was thinking more in a sexual way, not familial. He liked when I wore my hair in pigtails, like most schoolgirl fantasies. However, he favored granny panties or the ones with characters on them over the Victoria Secrets underwear. I would buy plenty of underwear from Victoria Secrets and although he never complained, he would rip them, so I wouldn't have them to wear again. If he didn't rip them, he would ruin them with baby oil. If it was something he liked, such as the granny panties or childlike underwear, he wouldn't destroy them. He would often ask about his favorite ones to see me wear. He told me one day that men don't like it when you look like you're trying to be sexy, so I shouldn't go buy that stuff (Victoria Secrets type lingerie). He said that men preferred when your panties don't match your bra and they like cotton, Walmart-type underwear instead, with turtles and other characters on them. So, that's what I bought from that point on.

That seemed to really turn him on tremendously. He didn't really take them off. He would perform oral sex with them on, he'd only just pull them to the side. I didn't completely get it as TV usually portrayed the opposite of what he said men actually like.

For as great as he was with words in his songs and music in general, he wasn't much of a conversationalist and the conversations he did have were not very mature. They consisted mostly of music, jokes, and sex-related topics. If he wanted to know what was going on in the world, he would ask me what I heard on the radio or have me read an article to him.

The only other thing he was highly fond of besides music, and sex, was basketball. He could play basketball from sun up to sun down. He'd always have to win though, no matter who he played. It was an unspoken rule. Even when he loss, he won. It was really weird, especially watching others give into him with no pushback. He did sign with a minor pro league back in 1997 for 2 years. He wore the number 12. He had a home gym with a basketball court in it at one of his homes. When he was out and about, Hoops was his favorite place to play. If he was out of town, he'd find a rec center or gym in the hood to go to, which is out of the norm for a celebrity, but he had his reasons.

Chapter 5

The worst and still unimaginable things he did to me under a cloak of deceit and manipulation still leaves me disgusted even now, to think about certain moments.

Early on in the relationship, he had approached me about having a threesome with one of his neighbors. He told me she was 16 years- old. Even though I was only 17, the scenario kind of put me off a bit, but we were close in age so maybe she had a birthday soon I thought. When I met her she looked older, as she was really more developed than I was in some areas. Reluctantly, I would still do this threesome for him.

It was kind of odd, because it was as if she already knew what to do. She knew exactly how to please him, and it was obvious this was not her first time. It is more likely, the two of them had maybe been together before. We had engaged in threesomes with this neighbor three times.

One occasion I remember vividly. We had just had a perfect night out a local radio awards show. I had a dress picked out especially for the event. He even faked an injury, so he didn't have to leave my side and perform. He gave everyone the night off after the event, so we could be alone on our drive back home. In my mind, this night couldn't be any more perfect. Just the two of us together in his Lincoln Navigator. His tags read "HOLY1" which was ironic because I thought that this night couldn't get any purer. It would be the most romantic night we've had in a while. I felt like a princess about to get her fairytale ending with her prince charming.

We parked on the side and walked arm in arm to the door. As soon as we crossed the threshold, he called the 16-year-old girl down from one of the guest rooms. Instantly, the smile that once graced my face, turned upside down. Then, it hit me, that this was why he sent everyone else home earlier. My heart dropped to the pit of my stomach. I couldn't believe he was about to ruin a perfectly good night.

It felt worse hearing the sound of him dragging this futon mattress from one room into his home gym as he summoned us both to follow him. Inside the home gym, he had a basketball court in which he decorated with a Space Jam theme. The theme that inspired him to write a song about him believing he could fly. To me, there was nothing inspirational about this moment especially hearing the sound the mattress made as it scrubbed the floor. He dragged this mattress into the middle of that court and set up his cameras around it. He would move back and forth to position the cameras or the mattress like a director aiming to get that perfect shot. This was another one of the times I cried uncontrollably. My crying only infuriated him because he said he couldn't use the footage for his perfect masterpiece he spent so much time setting up the camera for. I just had to get through it. I just wanted it to be over before it ever began.

The lights in the gym were so bright that the glare hurt my eyes. It was like many spotlights shining down upon us. He told the both of us to strip down. At this point, I was so sad and mad inside, so I was really not in the mood and it showed on my face. Looking over at her, she looked numb; emotionless. She just did as she was told, kind of like a programmed robot. I could also see she was wearing the same type of cotton underwear; the ones he liked and was highly turned on by.

He started off just pleasuring himself as he double and triple checked to make sure everything was set up properly. Because he knew I was upset, he made sure to pay special attention to me; trying to please me and get me in the mood. It didn't work. I couldn't forgive the fact that he had built me up that night only to crush me in the end. He spoke commands to both of us to position ourselves certain ways. He had sex with her, making her call him "daddy" just as he did me. The night ended with the both of us moaning, louder and louder as he commanded. The moaning turned him on. For him, it was both the sound of an audience for his performance and sweet symphony to his ears. While we were moaning he was bringing himself to a climax until he reached his peak.

Sometime after the third encounter (all the encounters happened over a 2-year span), the crying I did back then seemed like nothing compared to the crying I wanted to do as I got the shock of my life.

We were both at one of his video shoots chilling when I noticed she (the girl I was told was his 16-year-old neighbor) was just excited about something. So, I asked her what all the excitement was about. She just casually mentioned that she was getting a PT Cruiser for her 16th birthday.

In my mind, I'm freaking out and trying to do some calculations at the same time, because he said she was already 16 at the time of the first threesome, as well as she seemed to know just as much as I did about how to please him. If she was having a 16th birthday soon that means she was only 14 at the time. Did she lie about her age or did he just lie to me? I believed the latter as I grew to learn how he operated within the relationship, plus I was only 17 when he started a relationship with me. I learned a lot of what I did learn after the fact, however.

I didn't want to freak out in front of her or anyone for that matter. I wasn't aware who knew or didn't know about what she was doing. Did her parents already know? I wasn't sure. No one talked to anyone about anything. All the yes-men around him wouldn't be of any help either. I didn't know what to do, but I felt for some reason I had to help him get better. I was convinced that over time, he would if I fixed him. I wanted to cry but I couldn't without making a scene. I never did any threesomes with him and her ever again. I can't honestly say today, that he never did it behind my back, but I was done with that situation. I never had any threesomes with him after that with anyone not 18 or older.

It was really, causing me to have a lot of turmoil inside. I just had to talk to someone. However, with all the people around him being mostly yes-men and basically orchestrating everything he wanted to put in play, I didn't know who that person would be. Then, his publicist, Regina came to mind. I would confide in her about him having sex with the 14-year-old.

I don't think she confronted him about it or if she told anyone else. I just had to talk to someone about it. That moment really changed the dynamic of our relationship, because it was revealed that he was deceitful and a manipulator that didn't mind having sex with someone that young. I wondered what else he was lying to me about.

Turns out the man I loved, was not rightfully mines to love at all.

One day during a recording session, one of the runners came in to deliver a message. The runner told him that his wife was on the line. I was frozen with shock and trying hard to hold back the tears. It was an uncovering of the lie he made me believe. How could I really be his girlfriend, if he already had a wife? I felt like nothing in that moment. He doesn't say anything to me in that instance, instead he grabbed the runner and pulled him out in the hallway in an angry manner. I could hear him cursing out the runner, that ironically, I never saw again.

There were no signs to me at all that he was married. There was no ring or sign of a ring. The only one he wore was the one he had on his pinky finger in a lot of his videos. We were together all the time from sun up to sun down. I would be with him in the recording studio asleep on the couch until he finished recording and we would go to bed together. We only be apart for maybe a few hours if he had an errand to run or I was at the mall. Other than that, we were two peas in a pod. Where was this wife during that time? I couldn't believe what I was hearing.

He for sure, had some explanation for it ready to tell me. He told me that she knew everything that was going on and was cool with all of it. He even gave me the number to their house saying I could call there anytime if I needed him and she would be okay with it. Testing him on it, I did call a number of times. One time, she did answer the phone. She asked who was calling and I told her my name. She asked was it for business or pleasure? I told her "pleasure" and she hung up the phone. I then called him on his cellphone to tell him what had just happened. I was wondering if I had caused any chaos by calling. He told me that she was cool about it and that she didn't even say anything to him about it at the time.

At this point, I was living with him. I was totally dependent on him and couldn't just up and leave with no money. If she was cool with him being with me all the time, then I had intending on staying. None of these were the smartest decisions I can tell you now with no problem. Back then,

I was just trying to make the best of the situation I was involved in.

From that point on, however, I believed the runners developed a code to tell him his wife was on the line. They would tell him he had an "important call" instead. He never really had to deal with anyone saying anything about anything nor did he tolerate it. If a chick or anyone subordinate to him in some fashion did test him, he would tear them down so bad in front of everyone and you would not see them around again.

One night, we were out with a group of girls at a club. One of the girls said something slick to him. He would not let her back on the bus. Instead he had someone give her cab money, but he left her behind in another town. It was hours away from where she was originally from and needed to get to.

For that reason alone, he intentionally chose not to mess with women who were loud or had a big mouth. They could potentially be the one to spill the beans on his antics he'd like to keep private.

I can't say at some point I didn't get slick with him too, but in that situation, I was highly inebriated. I had liquid courage on my side.

One such memorable moment took place on the day we attended a party on a yacht. He didn't want me to mingle, so instructed me to just sit at the table and if I needed anything either he or his assistant would get it. Testing that theory and being agitated because I had to just sit at the table, I requested shots of Hennessey. No one would check for my ID anyway. By the time we made it off the yacht, I was really tipsy. Alcohol is a bit of a truth serum, and at that moment I felt compelled to speak the truth on what I had been holding inside. That night, we probably got into one of the biggest arguments we had. I was talking cash shit about him, how I felt about some of the things that had occurred between us, or the things he did.

Once we made it back to his studio, he had someone take me to one of the rooms upstairs which was like a mini apartment because it had a kitchen, bathroom and a bed. I was locked away there to sit alone by myself. I could hear voices and music coming from another room below, which sounded very much like a party to me. They were laughing and having a good time while I was stuck in this room. It made me angry, so I called down to the studio several times, but he didn't answer, nor did he come to the room. Being that I was fueled with anger and liquid courage at this point, I decided, it would be a good idea to play frisbee with some of his plaques on the wall. I tore some of them down and threw them across the room, which made a loud enough noise for others to hear. I remember clearly it was the plaques for the group, Changing Faces, and the soundtrack for "Don't be a Menace While Drinking Your Juice in the Hood". I was the menace that night that had drunk too much brown juice and the faces of those plaques were cracked, and on the floor. Pure savagery!

The security guard that was outside of my door let him know what I was doing. The security then let me know that his wife was also there in another room, and that I needed to be quiet. I told the guard that I didn't care about that because she knew about me. So, I kept making noise. He finally made his way to the room and we got into another argument. My mouth didn't care what it said. I told him the people downstairs didn't really care about him and then told him they only come around because of who he is, to which his reply was to throw water in my face.

The next morning, I woke up really afraid. The night before during the argument, he had talked about sending me back to Georgia and I boldly told him to do what he has to do. I was basically calling his bluff, plus I ripped his plaques off the wall. I didn't recall everything I said to him, but I just know it was very heated. However, once I got up he had someone tell me that he wanted to see me in the studio.

I was afraid to go because I was sure he was about to send me back considering what had took place. Most people around him were yes-people and never stood up to him. If they did, they were probably replaced.

When I got to the studio he played a song for me that he wrote. It was called, "I Don't Mean It". He told me that he wrote that song because when he "hollers at me" or "pull silly stunts", he doesn't mean it. This song was a way for him to try to make up with me for how he treated me. A lot of his songs were based on his experiences. How he treated me was foul, but the way I acted was also foul, I admit. After hearing the song, and him sing it to me, I wasn't as mad as I was before.

That was his M.O. typically. He never really outright said he was sorry, nor addressed the situation as to really communicate about the issues. He would always make it appear as if he went out of his way to smooth it over and the things he did to you were very minor in comparison and that's how he would have you see it. Kind of how a physically abusive partner will buy gifts. He'd write a song, sing you a song or he'd bring some celebrity around just to smooth things over to make you forgive him faster and without an actual apology.

Our trauma and talking about our trauma, was a commonality that bonded us together but in hindsight it was also a way for him to further dig his hooks into me, playing on my vulnerabilities and insecurities. I had told him about the sexual abuse I experienced as a young child, which in turn made him open up about his own repeated sexual abuse at the hands of his sister that went on for years. He said she at one point had him stick a pencil inside her and they would perform sex acts on each other. This same sister was still calling him and asking him for money as if nothing ever happened. Oddly enough, he exhibited the same pattern of behavior; never acknowledging the things he did wrong to you, expecting you too to just move on as if nothing ever happened. He would also confide in me about other things, which made me feel comfortable with him.

Some things he confessed, had me giving him the side eye. He told me that some time before he actually started having sex with girls he really wanted to have sex with, he would get his sister's sexy underwear and put them on. He would then go to the mirror and jack off at the reflection of his own ass. He did have a big butt for a man. It was a bit narcissistic in a twisted kind of way.

He also told me that he was really married to Aaliyah in 1994, when she was just 15-year-old. I had heard rumors but wasn't fully sure of the details. I asked him if they really forged the information on the marriage certificate. He said that they did do that in order for the marriage ceremony to take place. The reason they married, was because she was pregnant at the time. He was also afraid that he would get in trouble, but if she was his wife, he'd most likely not. They got the marriage annulled after she got the abortion and at her family's urging. He also told me the reason her family never spoke out was due to the fact that the mom was sexually attracted to him as well. Plus, he would sometimes sleep with her mother behind her back. He told me he used to visit them in Detroit and once the singer would go to sleep, he and the mother would have sex in the living room.

Neither of them ever really talked about their relationship while they were together nor when they split. He told me they had a pact; "Pins in Eyeballs". It meant that even if they had pins stuck in their eyeballs, they still wouldn't speak about their relationship to others.

All these things he would share to make you feel closer to him or feel the need to stick by him, nurture him even. It was all a game even though his pain may have been real. The pleasure was watching you eat up every word and be more than ready to overlook any wrong he was doing and participate in the antics that ran through his devious mind.

Chapter 6

There were good times in the relationship. The worst parts were mostly related to the sexual components. Outside of that, he was the charming, fun guy most people who didn't have sex with him knew and loved.

Outside of the threesomes, it was mostly just me and him during the course of the relationship. Even after threesomes, the girls would have to leave, or we would leave them. He liked when it was just him and I in the normal day-to-day routine. I was the only one he felt he could trust because I didn't want anything from him.

Since, I was the one person he trusted, and we were an item, he decided to use me for a lot of the things he had going on like videos or being a stage plant for his tours. I would be the girl he would pull up on the stage every time after he performed "Half On A Baby".

In 1999, I was on one of those tours with him, known as the "Get Up On A Room" tour. Several other artists were also performing throughout the leg of the tour. The lineup included rappers Nas and Foxy Brown as well as R&B singers, Kelly Price and Deborah Cox. So, it was the type of show that definitely drew a crowd. On that tour, he had a scene in the finale of his part of the show where there was a bed that appeared in the middle of the stage.

After he had finished singing one of his songs and was gearing up for the final song, he would sing the phrase "who wants to know what it feels like to be in my bed?" He would repeat that a few times to each side of the crowd. Then he would pan the audience on all sides of the room as if he was searching the crowd for someone. In the meantime, you'd just hear women screaming as he looked in their direction. The spotlight would shine on me and I'd give my best surprised but excited reaction. He told me to just cover my face and shake a little to help with my ability to act surprised. Security would then come to rush me on stage like we practiced several times before in rehearsal with his band and backup dancers in Gary, Indiana.

Once I got onstage, the first thing he would ask in particular, was my age and I would respond with "19" (but I was really 18). "19?" he would repeat back into the microphone. Then, we would pretend to be carrying on a conversation as if he was asking me other things, but he really wasn't. At some point after the fake conversation, a bed would appear on the stage, then I would strip down to those same underwear with the characters on them and non-matching black bra, while he was singing the melody. Can you imagine being up onstage in front of a room full of people with turtles on your drawers or the girl who got passed over for the girl with the childlike characters on her underwear? In the beginning, I would wear some lingerie, but he thought that looked too staged. He would always be wearing some see-through pajama pants with the see-through shirt, though.

We would get in the bed and we would simulate a love-making session. He would start to kiss me, then he would move further down. I would push his head down, but at that point he would raise up to look at the audience and then pull the covers over us. Although, at some of the shows, he actually was performing oral sex on me, unbeknownst to the audience because he was turned on by turtles on my underwear. Other times, we would just be under the covers being silly as we punched and kicked the covers up to further simulate lovemaking until the lights went out. We would be out of the bed and off the stage before the lights fully came back on.

I also remember during the tour Foxy Brown went from one of my top female rappers to one of my top haters.

During the tour, she made a habit of telling front row guests that I would be the one chosen. I couldn't wrap my head around why she was intentionally ruining the show. Even with her dating Kurupt and having a certified platinum album, she still was acting as if she was jealous. For what? She's been known to have her pick of celebrity men, so why was she so obsessed with little ole me?

I later asked Rob about the situation and why is it she was behaving that way. According to him, she wanted to be the one chosen. She wanted him to test drive the "Ill na na". She longed to be the one he was spending his time with after the shows, but I was in the way. If that wasn't enough, she proceeded to act childish at the hotel where we were all having an afterparty, after a show in Detroit. She just kept riding up and down the elevator with her security, which were two big, fat dudes. That was probably another sore spot for her. I, a non-celebrity, had more security than she did.

She rode the elevator continuously, hoping Rob would have noticed her and invited her to the party, but he didn't. At some point on her way up, a friend and I tried to get on the elevator. She quickly pushed the button to close the door and said "Nope! No scrubs!" as it closed shut. That situation still makes me laugh like hell. I was the scrub at the penthouse that she couldn't, but wanted to get in. The Chyna doll was acting more like a Bratz doll while she was on the tour.

Inside the penthouse party, there were women everywhere, which was common for the kind of parties he would have and really it was reflective of his everyday life. There would usually be little to no men there at his parties, but for this one, he did things a little differently. I recall him mentioning once, that Nick Cannon always wanted to come to one of his parties, but he never invited him. He considered Nick to be someone he considered a lame. Nas was in attendance because he was on the tour, plus some NBA players and several other entertainers I can't recall, but still, mostly women.

I remember those two the most because there was some interaction. A couple of the girls and myself had gathered in this jacuzzi tub that was in the penthouse. We were in our bathing suits having fun. I was sure to stay with the girls, to ensure he wouldn't see me talking with any of the guys. He came over at some point and began to pour baby oil on us and we were dancing as we lathered it all over. Somehow both Nas and one of the players ended up around the tub, taking in the view. They were trying to consort with me and one of the other females. Nas leaned in as to make small talk with me, but I had to nip that in the bud really quick and tell him I was with Rob, so there wouldn't be any issues. It was a fun party overall.

MTV news reported on the tour and the scene I was featured in. "The fan must have put in her 50 percent" is what they printed. So, despite a hater's attempts, it meant I was still pretty convincing.

When the tour was in Florida, he had us visit a lady's house by the name of Ms. Pat. She had such a beautiful home. We parked the tour bus and went swimming in her pool. She made us all feel welcomed with a plate full of pasta. We also watched videos of the tour while we were there as well. After filling our bellies and reliving moments of the tour, we would soon be on our way and on to the next city.

Other than fun while touring, there would be other moments. We often had roasting sessions that would be hilarious and lots of fun. He also made up a game where he would make a drink concocted of various things. He would put money down for the winner who could manage to drink it all. Those would be fun to watch.

He'd have parties in between touring that turned into a full-blown concert. DJ Wayne Williams and I would serve as backup dancers, while he would be tipsy performing his songs. Since I often practiced with them, I knew all the moves.

I recall one of the biggest and craziest parties that he threw in Olympia Fields at his mansion. It was a huge house party. Everyone had to leave their cellphones at the door in a basket. The power was turned off on each phone by whomever had the basket. So, what went on at the house party stayed there. They didn't get their phone back until the party was over.

The goal was to try to get everyone to stay up the entire weekend. He had invited a ton of women of course. Of his celebrity friends, he invited Baby, his brother Slim and an R&B singer signed to their label, named TQ. We all hung out and had a good time. The others were mixing and mingling but I remained close to him. I still had a good time. The guests did a lot of bike riding, roller skating, dancing, swimming, and we even had a fashion show. Whatever you had to do to stay up the whole weekend, that's what you did.

For the fashion show portion of the party, he had all the girls go to the mall and buy something for the fashion show. Everyone would model what they purchased. He cracked jokes on some of the outfits, which made everybody laugh. There were a few moments of drama but just normal stuff that happens when you get a bunch of catty females in one room. It didn't last long though.

No one lasted the whole time. People were dropping like flies everywhere. They were asleep on the couch, in the bathrooms, on the floors, by the pool, anywhere they ended up when sleep overtook them.

He once was generous enough to make sure his male staff received a "special treat". He typically does not allow consorting between any of the girls and the men who were around. However, if it was girls that he didn't know, he didn't much care. He decided to concoct a plan to make sure his "boys" got sexed one night after a show. He told me the plan beforehand and how he was going to pull it off. I thought he was out of his mind when I heard it, but I just played along.

Rob had invited some girls he considered groupies to the tour bus to party, he decided they would fit the plan perfectly. He told me that once everyone got on the bus that we would go to the bed and pretend to start having sex, which in turn would make the rest of the partygoers do the same. Sounds crazy, right?

Well, once everyone was on board and chilling, he pretended to kiss me. Then he proceeded to feel me up and we started fake humping. To my surprise, the mood we created started to spread, except they were going a bit further. We excused ourselves from the bus and left them to their tour bus orgy. The guys were able to enjoy themselves that night, but usually he didn't treat them right or pay them well. Fun was definitely had by all. Unfortunately, for the girls, they were booted off the tour bus with all their belongings as they ate their breakfast at I-hop the next morning, but not without cab fare, which he provided.

These were the times he was at his best and it was the side that pulled people into whatever web he wanted to weave, and it was a way for him to smooth over the shitty way he'd often treat them before.

SCENES FROM THE TOUR BUS

You'd think this was the outcome of having multiple people on the tour bus. Nope, just one. He'd leave such a mess that I'd have to clean up before I could find a space to sit down.

Chapter 7

Sometimes the highest highs are followed by the lowest lows. It's a cycle of life many sometimes do not recover from.

After the tour was over, we resided at the Trump International in New York for about a month. During our time there, he would have a nervous breakdown. He didn't have the desire to sing anymore. He cancelled all his interviews and other shows he was scheduled to do while there in New York. He wasn't answering any phone calls, either. He was done.

He told me that he just wanted to get away from everything. He ended up sending everyone home, with the exception of me and Frank Gatson, his choreographer at the time. He didn't send Frank home, because he would be the one to get us the rooms and do all the footwork. The room we ended up getting for the night was at a real roach motel. It looked like it had rats and probably did. It was definitely a hole in the wall type of place. This new location would also be the last place people would suspect that he is staying in while there in New York.

He ended up shaving all the hair off his face and head. He bought a Jamaican dreadlock wig that came with a colorful beanie attached to it and some headphones to help keep him in disguise. We walked through New York city train station without people recognizing him. We took the train from New York to Chicago. From Chicago we went to California on the California Zephyr train. It was probably one of the most peaceful trips I'd been on with him. The scenery was nice, there were no other women, no media, the pace was slow, and the mood was normal. It was just us.

All the while, his publicist was constantly calling both our phones and other people to find him. He wasn't ready to be found yet. We ended up at a ski resort at Lake Tahoe. We stayed there for another month. He recorded in a small studio and was working out regularly. We'd go to the movies and just chill at the resort. He just needed the time away from it all to regroup and renew himself.

I finally reached out to his publicist, due to the fact that she and I had gotten really close over the years I had been dating him. She was the only female I could really talk to on a daily basis and she would typically be the one to handle things if I needed my hair done or a dress for an event. She was the closest thing to a friend that I had, and I didn't want to keep her in such a panicked state for so long. I told her where we were because at least for business purposes she would know how to handle the situation.

Once he was ready to go back, we left and returned home. Everything went back to the way it was. He was in the studio again and it was a steady groove into the year 2000, until it wasn't.

I missed my period! So, I quickly took a pregnancy test to see if I was actually pregnant or not. The test came back positive. It was not the right timing and definitely not the best of situations to bring a kid into. I had to find the nerve to tell him because I didn't know how he would respond. When I did finally tell him, he had me take another test in front of him.

That test also came back positive. My anticipation was for him to become enraged, but he actually had the exact opposite demeanor when I told him the results. He just asked me what I wanted to do.

It surprised me that he was actually giving me an option instead of telling me what was going to happen. I told him that I wanted an abortion. I simply was not ready and also in the back of my mind I knew there was indication that he could possibly be into younger girls. I didn't want to take the chance on having a girl. He seemed okay with my decision. However, he also seemed to just forget that I was even pregnant at times. He let it linger on for a while, at least until I reached 3 months before he decided to make sure I got to the clinic.

It was almost as if he wanted to keep it, because I had to be the one to remind him. At times, I was too sick to go anywhere, so I would just stay in my room. He moved me to the Ritz-Carlton inside the Water Tower suite. He then started to work from the room instead of going to the studio or wherever else he needed to go. He had everyone come there. His stylist was in one room, his staff in another downstairs and he would conduct interviews and photoshoots in the kitchen area and other parts of the suite.

Although he never really said if he wanted me to keep the baby or not, he just behaved differently than I'd expect. He could have wanted me to keep it or just wanted to keep an eye on me. I'm not 100% sure either way, but I was definitely clear about what I had decided to do. He didn't schedule it until I finally brought it back up again.

His assistant, June, made the appointment for me within a week and posed as my uncle when we had to fill out the paperwork because I needed a driver home after the procedure and a family member poses no red flags. I was actually further along then I realized. I thought I was 12 weeks, but the doctor told me I was actually 13 1/2 weeks, which costed more than what was paid earlier in the appointment, but she was nice enough to let it slide.

I threw up one last time after the procedure, but after some ginger ale, soup, and crackers I was better. I was taken back to my room in the suite and there I laid in the bed alone. After a week had passed, that's when he called to check on me to see how I was doing. I told him I was doing much better, which I was since I was no longer pregnant. He asked if I wanted to come to his video shoot. I agreed to come just to get out of the room and to check out what he was doing.

We met up in the trailer on the set of the "I Wish" video. He told me he wanted me to be in this video. He had talent there, but he didn't want to use them because he wanted the elements of the video to appear more natural and they were too made up for the look he was trying to achieve. I ended up being the girl on the porch braiding his hair.

I attended the "Fiesta" Remix video shoot in Miami that year as well. I watched as Jay Z, Dame Dash and Memphis Bleek shot their scenes. Boo, Gotti and Blackie were also in the video and they're good friends of mine still, even to this day. Rob didn't want me to be in this video because it was a lot of other male celebrities in it. As I sat on the sidelines watching them record, he kept a close eye on me.

Little X and his team were at the shoot. He wanted to book me as talent for future jobs, but before I could utter a word, his PR team stepped in to shut that down. He would do things like that. As if there was only room for his star to shine plus it was a way to make sure that he would remain the source for what you needed. Any normal person wouldn't have a problem with you making your own money.

At the time, I was staying at the Peabody Hotel. They had an event called "March of the Ducks". It's a 1930's tradition that had trained ducks marching from a fountain in the hotel onto a strip of red carpet. These ducks were guided by their Duckmaster and sometimes volunteers from the audience to a lift or elevator and raised up to the rooftop. They would remain there until it was time for them to come back down to the fountain to do it once more.

When I was at the vacation home in Orlando that he got for me, I convinced him to let my cousins come visit because I was in this big house all by myself and they would be able to keep me company while he was away. He agreed with my reasoning for the invitation, then June made the arrangements.

He flew them down for a week. My cousins were used to doing whatever they wanted to do. So, they would look at me crazy when I went to call Rob before I even made a move to go somewhere. They weren't in a controlling relationship, so they didn't have that notion. When they would sporadically leave the house, it would stress me out because I didn't have the control over the situation in Rob's absence. I wasn't the one doing it, but just to have them do it was enough. We did manage to have some fun though.

Unfortunately, my cousin got sick while she was there. She had a flare up of her sickle cell anemia. She told me that the staff was treating her badly so, Rob and I visited her at the hospital on our way to the club to lift her spirits and see if we could tip things in her favor. She said the hospital staff definitely treated her better after seeing him and his entourage come to visit her.

I missed them when they left to go home. I cherished the moments we did spend together.

(At the Florida vacation home with my cousins)

(I was so happy when my cousins came to visit me. It lifted
my spirits to be with family.)

Chapter 8

Here I am. The big 2-1; a milestone for most.

At 21-years-old is when most people start to develop some sort of vision for their life, outside of the partying and utilizing every bit of their newfound legal drinking status. I have lived the life of an adult at a young age and drinking was already checked off my list. I wanted something more, a vision for my future like everyone else. Kicking it every day in the studio and having numerous threesomes was not the life I envisioned for myself in the future. Sometimes a tiny voice inside you will let you know when it's time to move and mines was screaming. I wanted better for myself. I wanted better for him too, but he didn't seem to want it for himself.

He showed no signs of changing anytime soon. Repeating the same things and hoping for a different result was perfectly clear to me at this time that it was insanity. It was time to go.

There were times I would go home periodically for a visit just to catch up with family and friends as well as get a break from the monotony. This time, I would go home, but not readily return.

Ironically, at this same time of my return home, news outlets were breaking the story of how they found this gym bag in Florida full of homemade child pornography belonging to the man I just left not too long ago. I was gaining my wings and his was being clipped. He was arrested and charged with 21 counts of manufacturing child pornography based on an investigation in Chicago plus 12 counts from Florida based on photos police allegedly found of him and underage girls being sexually active. Turns out they had been investigating him for years prior and a Chicago Sun-Times reporter received the first of 2 videotapes from an unknown source that he had turned over to police the year before. The second tape he received that year is the one that caused the indictment because it contained the 14-year old, that I was told was 16 years old when I met her.

I didn't know what to think or how to feel. I was just numb at the situation. I still loved him, but love could not cover that. I realized I had to focus on my own life. He posted bail just days later. The charges in Florida were dropped. He made a lot of people a lot of money, I was sure that between them and him, he had it covered. It was time for me to venture into a new beginning.

Chapter 9

The first thing I did when I got back home in commemoration of my 21st birthday was bought myself a drink, legally. It was an Amaretto Sour. Drinking legally, is the big to-do at this age, but I had experienced that already, so that excitement was short-lived. I did, however decide it was time for me to attempt to get "back to normal" and for me that meant enjoying this pivotal moment in my life.

I was going to make up for all the lackluster birthday celebrations I had prior. I partied like a caged bird that was now free. I had lots of fun with my friends intending to live my best life. Things were looking better for me and I was certainly in a better place mentally.

During a night on the town with friends and partying at Club Cream in Atlanta, I met my first boyfriend that would soon be my daughter's father. When we first met, we connected instantly. We had breakfast after a night of partying. We kind of stuck to each other like glue afterwards.

Dating as an adult is definitely a lot less simple compared to the dates I used to go on as a young teen in middle school. The best date I had ever went on was my very first date. We only went to the movies and got something to eat, but it was the innocence of it all that made me cherish it the most. It was pure and sweet. This felt pretty close, at least in the beginning.

This new romance was on the fast track and running hot and heavy. We eventually, ended up moving in together and not long after, I became pregnant 4-5 months later with my first daughter. I wasn't looking to have a kid this time around either but the feelings of having a "normal life" had me locked in for the ride. It was "girlfriend to a guy that worked as a barber and we were expecting a baby" kind of normal. I was basking in every minute of it.

Then, all of a sudden, something changed. Pregnancy typically brings couples close together, and the man usually takes extra care with the woman who is having his baby. Somewhere along the line, a flip switched, and he became a terror. Instead of massages and backrubs, I got tackles and punches. I don't know what could make a person, just change up that quickly and without warning. It is typically, something internal they are fighting with but expressing the rage in a physical way. I felt like he may have been struggling to be whom he really was inside, rather it be fear, shame or pressures of society. However, it's still no excuse to be abusive. If my pregnancy with his child didn't keep him from putting his hands on me, there is really not many boundaries left to cross after that which would not leave me in an even worse position.

I had to figure out how to get out of that situation for my child's sake as well as my own. I couldn't leave right away, as I was in a dependent state and had no income of my own. I decided to stay until my daughter was born. Once she was born, I figured out an exit strategy.

I had to be anywhere but there, so I decided to see if I could possibly go back to Chicago for a little bit just to get away. So, I decided to reach out to the publicist that would help me get the things I needed when I was living in Chicago, to test the waters a bit. I knew that I had left there at such a pivotal moment and wasn't sure how I would be received. She would be the one who would know best if he was willing to hear from me or not.

I called her kind of nervously, not knowing what to expect but to my surprise she said he had been looking for me for a long time. She stated she wanted to call him to let him know she found me and that she would call me right back. That phone call put me on my way to Chicago but with a small addition. While my daughter's father was at work, he had a car sent to pick up me and my baby to take us to the airport where we made our getaway to Chicago.

At this point in time, I was between two relationships in which I had no closure on because I had to make a break for it. The first one would serve as a temporary safe haven for the second one, which sounds a bit crazy given the history and his last arrest. The key word is temporary, because I was carrying around precious cargo.

Once I got to Chicago, I was met by him and Derrel McDavid, his accountant. They wanted me to do a blood test to see if my daughter was in fact, his daughter. I told them there was no need for that because it would be impossible for me to carry a baby that long given when I left and how old my daughter was at the time. In all honesty, I didn't expect him to be that cool with me popping up with a kid that wasn't his, but he was very cool about it.

We would remain in Chicago for a little while. In the midst of being there, I had to get shots for my daughter, but they would also test her for lead since the pipes there was so old. They were one of the only places I knew that did that for babies. I had my daughter with me as I moved around. I was going to be the only one to care for her.

He was cool with me bringing her around, but it got a bit weird for me when he would always want me to put her in dresses. He would literally give me money to go buy her some dresses when I would dress her in leggings and clothes that were more suitable for the cold Chicago weather. It was too cold for that kind of attire, but since he was convinced that she should be wearing dresses since she was a little girl, he would insist on me buying them. It was probably totally innocent, but being her mother and given his past decisions, I wasn't willing to risk it. I had to protect my daughter by all means.

We would leave Chicago not too long after and head back home to Georgia. I did return periodically, but for short periods of time and never with her. A relationship is very unhealthy when you can't trust the other individual with anything. The older I got, the less I would see him and the less I wanted to have sex with him. It got to the point where I just wanted to hang as two friends, without the benefits. All the extra women had become too much, and his lack of condom usage was too high a risk to be involved with sexually. It was safe to consider it a wrap. The last time we had a sexual encounter would be in 2007.

We were still friends and he would help me if I needed it. After I had returned home with my daughter, he still cared for me. He helped me get around with my daughter by buying me a car. Of course, he didn't buy it directly, but he did do some research for one, he had June make sure I got the money order he sent to purchase the vehicle, a Ford Mustang, in cash.

For me, the friendship ended with the last Thanksgiving I spent with him at his home in Olympia Fields. While I was there, he told me Rashona said to tell me "hello". I was a bit surprised, so I asked where she was at now. He told me that she was staying in one of his guest rooms while wearing a sick smirk on his face. Rashona was the neighbor he told me was 16-years-old when she ewas really 14-years-old. Even though, at this point she was now a grown woman, I had hoped that all those years that he stopped messing with her. I was sadly mistaken. That was the straw that broke the camel's back for me. After years of trying to help him change, I realized he was sick and beyond the help that I could give him. It broke my heart his sick and deceptive ways is what caused us to part. This was no longer someone I could be friends let alone lovers with.

This same year, I met my second child's father. I thought he was great to be around until I realized how self-centered he was in reality.

Mistakenly, I had confided in him during the course of the relationship about my past relationship with the Rob. I also told him that I asked a friend to stash away a tape I had stumbled across a while back that contained myself engaged in sexual activity. I told him the guy was speaking to some people who were trying to get him to sell the tape, but I didn't want it to be sold. I didn't want myself out there like that for the world to see. After I told him, it really put a damper on our relationship. He asked me for his number one day. I thought maybe he was just feeling a little insecure and if I give him the number, the insecurity would subside. I thought it would assure him I that he was the only person I was dealing with. However, I didn't think that he would call the number.

The next day when I came over to visit him, I was just in shock. He told me that he actually called and on top of that, he told him that I had the tape. I didn't understand why he would do that? Most importantly, why did he do it to me? Even if he was trying to get one up on him, he threw me under the bus in the process. He put himself in the center of a situation that had nothing to do with him. I wanted to deal with it in my own time, but he forced my hand.

When I went to Chicago, I was a bit nervous even though he asked me to come. He wasn't too bothered by the situation, even though my boyfriend calling him made the situation seem fishy. Myself and the person that I gave the tape to had to take a lie detector test when we met up with him. There were steps we had to go through that I attribute to my then boyfriend inserting himself into something he had no business getting involved in.

The lie detector test was to prove that the tape really existed and if so, whether or not we made copies. His accountant was the one who had us take it at the lawyer's office. I passed my test, but my friend failed his when it came to the question of if copies were made. So, we had to return another day because the accountant told my friend he wouldn't receive full compensation until all the copies were brought to him. Rob had offered us $250,000 for the tape's return. The accountant decided he would make us split the amount of $200k and the last $50,000 would be paid after the trial. He also paid the upfront amount in portions. The first visit he paid us $20,000. The second visit, my friend got paid $80k after he passed the lie detector test and he did not have to come back anymore.

As for me, the accountant fixed it to where I would have to come back a third time. It irked my nerves because originally, I was told to oversee the situation since we were once in a relationship, we weren't blackmailing him, and he never knew me to do anything shady. However, the accountant muscled his way in to take over. In two visits, he had given me half of what he gave my friend. He made me take a lie detector on the third visit, but he didn't ask "yes" or "no" questions as if to purposefully make me fail. "How much money do you have in your bank account?" is not the type of question asked during these tests. He was purposefully being a dick asking me these types of questions. So, I failed it of course.

He just needed a reason to be upset. He even had the nerve to threaten me as if I did anything wrong to him personally. This guy was obviously into more than just accounting. He had personally sat down and watched the tape in our presence, which is not something a professional accountant would do; he would just handle the money. While watching the tape, he wasn't interested in the parts in which I was filmed, just the parts when the underage girl called his client "Daddy" and specifically referred her to her "14-year-old p-ssy". That's the part of the video that made it important for him to get the tape back. That phrase was repeated by the both of them at least 6 times. If the phrase wasn't enough to make you sick, he also urinated on her. This 14-year-old girl was the same girl he told me was 16-years-old; 2 years before she actually turned 16. This was a different tape from the one he would be on trial for.

Derrel told me that he should have "murked" me from the beginning. He said it as if there had been prior conversations about this even before today. I was not trying to hold the tape over anybody's head, I just didn't want my image out there like that. I wasn't doing anything for him to put a hit out on me. I also was not physically holding the tape and hadn't held it until I gave it to my friend. I had to figure out a way to protect myself.

I contacted the prosecution in the case they were trying to hide evidence from to do the right thing as well as create a safeguard for myself and my children. I didn't know what this accountant was capable of doing, so I needed to let it be known that there was a plan to kill me so that it would be on public record and decrease the chances of it actually happening. I felt that it would be safer to tell the truth and to tell my story of what actually happened.

As it turned out, my instincts were right. It was rumored that there were ties to the mob. The famed Chicago-Sun Times reporter who had received the anonymous videotape and testified at the trial stated that he was threatened by a former business manager. He said someone called him in the midst of the trial claiming that they knew he had a daughter as if to say they would possibly harm her just to shut him up. The day after the Sun-Times ran the story about the videotape he said someone shot out a front window at his home.

I definitely did the best thing for me and my kids in that moment.

Chapter 10

Months later and a bundle of joy in the belly, I made my way through the media circus and into the courthouse.

June 3, 2008 was my day to testify in this trial that had started days prior. It's been 6 years in the making due to much of the defense lawyers' strategic maneuvering, but there finally was a trial. The lawyers did everything they could to hold off the trial. During that time, the judge, who was friends with the defense counsel, somehow injured his leg and instead of replacing the judge, they insisted on waiting for him to heal. Now the girl, who was once a minor, is now a young adult and the allegations are no longer fresh in a lot of the public's minds. The testimonies and lines of questioning that took place would heavily shape the case. Tense but weird vibes in the air the whole time.

The day I took the stand, was a day I'll never forget. I was nervous, not about my testimony, but about these lawyers whom he had hired. If they could hold off a trial this long with no recourse, what other tricks did they have up their sleeves?

Usually during cross-examination, they would ask you questions relating to the defendant. That day, this was not the case. The defense attorney made sure I felt like I was the one on trial instead of his client. He asked if it were true that my kids' fathers were felons, then proceeded to tell me that's all I dated (never mind the fact that I also dated their client). I was called a street walker and the devil. His words were that the devil will come to you in the form of an angel in regard to me. They were constantly attempting to make their client look like the victim.

They tried to brand me as a gold digger and a thief by claiming that I stole his watch. He and I both knew that I didn't steal the watch. He had only forgotten where he left it. He had flown back to Chicago one day from Atlanta and left the watch with me. I could have told him I had it. I just wanted to see how long it would take him to figure out where he left it. It pissed me off that he didn't know. Even with knowing there were other girls he was messing with the same time we were dating, this made me think I wasn't aware of the magnitude of how many there were. On top of that, he never brought it up again because he most likely had insurance on it. So, it was not as significant at that time as they tried to make it appear in court.

It was clear all he cared about was saving his own skin. I mean, he was willing to let the blame be put on his brother, knowing he had nothing to do with the case at all. Not to mention, he had paid my oldest daughter's father $50,000 to make up lies on me and try to destroy my credibility. It's sad when money can make you sell out the mother of your own daughter.

Their (his lawyers') overall tactics were to discredit me as a witness and create a distraction to the case at hand. They asked me nothing about their client.

I felt they needed to make that connection clear, which was the reason I was there to further speak to the validity of the tape. It was 3 hours of everyone talking about me when the focus should have been elsewhere. I addressed my concerns with the prosecution before I even took the stand. I didn't have any intentions on lying. I knew they would bring up the watch in an attempt to tarnish me. I felt that the prosecution addressing it, made me look more like a criminal when the question only required a simple "yes" or "no" before they moved on to the next question. I wasn't concerned about how I looked at the time, I only testified because it was the right thing to do and because my life had been threatened in the midst of this chaos.

I didn't consider myself when I first took the stand, but my lawyers thought that I should and suggested that I seek an immunity deal, because after his trial ended, they may still seek to go after me for what I just testified to under oath. It didn't matter if I didn't know and since I gave my friend the tapes in Chicago and he took it with him back to Kansas City, Missouri they could bring up charges if they wanted. I did end up getting both federal and state immunity, thankfully.

The whole ordeal was just stressful on top of being pregnant. The outcome was not surprising to me at all. He had confided in me a while back about hiring some lawyers he called his "dream team" and that is exactly what they turned out to be. They succeeded in keeping the trial date delayed long enough to create doubt as to who it was on the tape. Also, the girl's parents and herself said the girl on the tape wasn't her. Many don't know that she was still with him before, during and after the trial. Her dad continued to play guitar for him for years after the trial.

Even with countless other people clearly identifying her by her voice, hairstyle and appearance, it was enough to create reasonable doubt in the jury pool. They returned a verdict of "not guilty". His fans that still believed in his innocence, the ones whom he made money for and ones that needed his money for survival all rejoiced.

His songs still played on the radio and he even put out a new song that won the people over. They were able to dance away any remnants of filth that came with this trial. Not to mention, the leaked video made him somehow more desirable to some in a lustful way. He went on to receive a NAACP Image Award and lots of praise. It's odd, because there was a time when the young starlet he married some time ago was about to receive an award and got booed off the stage. Two separate events with him, the master manipulator, at the center, but in both cases, the victims got the short end of the stick. To bring it all full circle, one of the fans waiting outside the courthouse in support of him was a young teen by the name of Jerhonda Pace, who would later become one of his underage victims of abuse.

Chapter 11

After the trial was over, I was ready to get back to my regular life. I was expecting my son soon. I got calls for interviews. I only did a few such as Warren Ballentine's show, Tom Joyner, and V103. I was tired of the spotlight though. I just wanted a bit of normalcy again.

My boyfriend felt quite the opposite. He wanted me to continue to do shows, photoshoots and other interviews. If I was in the limelight, then so was he by proxy. That's where he liked to live, under the glow of it all. He became mad at me because I stopped doing shows and he had enough of me "passing on opportunities". Eventually, I'd had enough too....of him. This would be the first relationship that I would officially end as opposed to the prior ones where I just abruptly left, or should I say, escaped. He cared more about the fame than my mental state.

The next situation- needless to say, I didn't have it my way, but he sure was reminiscent of the Burger King man (he was quite the character) making sure all eyes were on him as he drew attention to himself. Even adorning himself at one point with a crown and dying his hair blonde. It should have been an easy red flag for me to pack up my little nuggets and run. I did, but just not as fast as I needed to.

Before I left, my affiliation with him led to a traumatic event that would leave a mental scar not only for myself but for my kids and my daughter's best friend as well. I remember it like yesterday, it was July 4th of 2016. He was away with one of his artists, and we were at home sleeping comfortably in our beds, when a group of men broke in. I woke up to glass breaking and I thought one of the kids, particularly my daughter, had broken a dish while late night snacking. In reality, it was the backdoor glass shattering. Thinking that it was just my daughter, I didn't move too quickly. I had barely opened my eyes to yell out to her and ask her what she broke, when I saw a gun in my face. The men were all wearing masks and ransacking the place as if they were looking for something. The guy with the gun told me to get down on the floor and lie face down. I'm terrified at this point because I didn't know what to do and I didn't want them to harm my baby that was still lying fast asleep in the bed.

As I was lying down on the floor, I was worried about my kids. What I didn't realize is that they heard the commotion and decided to hide in a closet. While in hiding, my daughter called 9-1-1 and was on the phone with them as this was taking place. I, on the other hand, was too afraid to move with the gun drawn on me. The guy proceeded to ask me where the guns and money were. I didn't know what he was talking about, so I told him just that. In the meantime, the others were searching desperately, and making a mess of things. Then, one guy stumbled across a gun in the closet, so this made the other guy think that I was lying. I told them that I didn't know that it was there.

The guy standing over me spotted my alarm system on the side of my bed and began to repeatedly tell me to turn it off. I told him I couldn't turn it off, hoping it will make them leave faster if they thought the police were on their way. However, the alarm was not on at the time. The other guys went upstairs and looked around but didn't find anything. To me, it seemed as if they had been there before. Especially, since the house sat by the lake and it was always pitch-black in the backyard and too dark to really see anything. You would have to know where you were going in order to move around that easily to find your way inside.

Not happy with what little they found, the guy threatened me. He asked me if I believed that he would kill me as if that would force me to tell them about the guns and money I knew nothing about. Then, he let off a shot by my head. My life flashed before my eyes seeing the hole the bullet made through the floor. I was thinking that this was going to be the way I would leave this earth; leave my kids behind. The shot also woke up my baby. Fortunately, she didn't cry, as I thought that would only aggravate them. I'm thinking she thought she was dreaming is why she didn't really make a sound. She just sat on the bed rubbing her eyes and staring at them.

They asked me again about money and guns. I told them I did have money in purse. It was a little close to $700. They went in my purse, took my money, my cellphone and my car keys. The guy told me to lie still on the floor as they made their way out. I waited until I didn't hear anything to finally get up off the floor. I grabbed my baby and went upstairs to the kids' rooms. I found my daughter and her friend in the closet. That's when I found out she had been on the phone with police for the last 8 minutes. The whole ordeal took place in 10 minutes but, it seemed like an eternity. We looked out the window, but we didn't see them. They were long gone, at least for that moment.

However, these were not the smartest criminals. They left their legally registered getaway car parked nearby with receipts for the Iphone that was just bought by one of the thieves. Both things registered to him in his real name. This was how they were able to at least track him down. The gas station he visited in the same car before coming to rob me, had cameras that provided police with the visual images they needed. In the end, this guy turned out to be my ex's friend. He is still waiting to go to trial and one of the guys hasn't been found yet.

Not even having his family going through an ordeal like that made him want to be a stand-up man. His justification for what he did was the fact that he always came back….. eventually. He behaved much like a bipolar narcissist. It's ironic that my past relationships were filled with a lot of selfish, narcissistic men. They had too much love for themselves and yet I didn't have enough.

The relationships we have in life are like mirrors. What we put up with and allow in them often reflect how we feel inside about ourselves and the energy we give off. Looking back on all of the tumultuous relationships I have had in my life from as early as 17, and up until my last child's father, I have to admit just as they didn't have a proper love for me, I really didn't have it for myself. Developing that love came with time, mistakes, self-awareness and correction.

I had to learn to love myself properly in order to open my eyes with the discernment to sense the bullshit. I stood my ground on what I would and would not accept in my life. I knew to cut things off once I got that "red flag" alert. There was no need for further discussion afterwards.

Developing self-love and self-awareness allowed me to be in a space where I was open to recognize and receive real love.

I finally met someone that wasn't controlling, manipulative, and I could 100% be myself around. He didn't make me feel afraid, insecure or bring me down.

I think the difference was that he came from a family where his parents were together and married his whole life. He had a strong foundation in and with his family. They had family reunions and other get-togethers. All the things, I didn't have growing up. I was overjoyed that I was able to give my kids a glimpse of a functional family through him. His father became the grandfather my kids needed. It's bittersweet to see what you missed in your own childhood, but your kids are able to have it. For that, I was happy and it's what counted the most; being able to give your kids better than what was given to you.

He also had two kids of his own. Two boys that were close in age to my son. So, he knew what it meant to be a parent already and it was a role he took seriously. Having a son, it is good as well as important, for him to be around positive men and for him to have other boys to hang out with. We blend well together.

There is no such thing as perfection, because there will always be ups and downs. We've both had to go through our own personal journeys in life to get to where we found ourselves and were ready for each other.

Chapter 12

Every now and then I would have people asking me questions about my life before and during the trial of 08'. I was in a good, peaceful place in my life, so I thought I could finally open up about the story of me, not just about my life with some famous singer with a lot of controversial issues, although he played an intricate part of it. I wanted to really focus on the cycles of abuse and how it happened in different forms in order to bring awareness and help others not only recognize it, but to also bring about the necessary steps for people to heal from it as well. However, I did want to make the misunderstandings or misconceptions that people had very clear.

I knew the media had did their best at slandering me and people were talking as if they knew everything. They tried to make it seem as if I wasn't in a relationship with him. Just because they didn't see me on camera, doesn't mean I wasn't there. From 98'- 01, I was either off to the side or front and center for most of the things he did. Such as the American Music Awards, where he and I both wore our hair braided to the back and dressed in all black. I remember waiting backstage and Andy Garcia walked up to me just to compliment my hair and look for that evening. So, I was there just as I was in his videos. His publicist said he was ready to risk it all that night. In the end, he would always put himself first.

Thinking about how to tell my story, I weighed my options. I wasn't really a big reader. I leaned more towards visuals on the screen, so instead of doing a book I decided I would embark on the path to making my own documentary. I would take people on a journey, showing them actual places that I landed in, such as the foster home on Capen Street, where I grew up when I was adopted, my aunt's place on 33rd and 4th in Minneapolis, Chicago Trax, and other places where things in my life happened. I wanted them to get the full picture and to dispel a lot of the rumors and misinformation.

As, I was gearing up to do the documentary, I got a phone call from a family that was now frantic because they were trying to get their daughter back. Their daughter was now with the man that I left behind in Chicago and had been with him for nearly two years. He, at this stage in life had a fully developed operation where he had several females in one dwelling place functioning as his sex slaves. He had basically escalated from the life he used to live. Reportedly some of the women had been there since they were as young as 14 years old.

The family had contacted me about being a part of a documentary series that they were doing. They needed someone from the past (the 90's) to further validate a pattern and to tie it all together. Especially, since I was the one to testify at the trial which is on public record. My participation would give them at least two of the time periods they needed to be covered. I did tell the production company that I was working on my own documentary. However, I agreed to come on board, because I believed it could help a lot of the victims as well as keep others from becoming potential victims. Many did not realize that there was an entire system at play. One that has had decades of practice and is comprised of different people in different roles but they all helped facilitate or enable his behavior. Some were outright complicit, and some, unwilling participants. The only person that was left in the dark was the victim, who often didn't see the light until it was too late, and they've already endured the trauma.

This moment in time, I believed people would be more receptive to hearing the truth, than when I first told it in 2008.

During the time leading up to the taping there were frequent phone conversations to keep me updated and in the know of the process (legalities, etc.) and also to make sure I was still on board with the project. I was also introduced to different staff members who worked with the company producing the documentary. Over time, there were also more stories coming to the surface and some involving the contraction of a disease as serious as herpes. This prompted me to get on the phone and reach out to his publicist, Regina, to see if this disease was present when I was with him. She confirmed that it was true, but somehow, I was definitely blessed enough not to carry anything or pass it along to my children. On top of that came a 19-minute song, admitting nothing but blaming others. In this song, I was addressed, not by name of course. He was cursing me out, but at the same time speaking on how he loved me, and how he bought me a car. Well, the exact words were:

"Bitch you know who you are
Bitch I bought you a car,
Bitch you stayed in my crib
I loved you with all my heart!"

He must have forgotten that I had once loved him too, but he abused and used that love to manipulate me in the worst way. There are some things in life that love will just not cover.

Looking back over the years, it definitely has been a long and rocky journey to get here. I would not have imagined being able to do what I wanted for so long on a platform that I was about to join forces with. To get to where I can make a difference to many other young girls that's like my former self as a teen, is amazing, but inside I fought hard to contain the turmoil.

Often when you speak on certain moments of your life, especially such as this, you relive everything; all the pain, shame, sadness and frustration. All the emotions hit you at once. Even though you are far from that moment, your brain can't comprehend a way to relay that to your heart to suppress your emotions.

This morning, I woke up with a bit of anxiety. I was ready to tell my story and to continue to bring awareness as I had already started doing before the documentary, but it's never really easy to tell it without emotionally putting yourself right back in that moment. I was determined to try my best for the sake of the girls whose families just wanted them back home, and for other abuse survivors like me, especially those who had to endure it early on in their childhood.

So, here I am. Ready for my close up. I have gone through the process of beautification both literally and symbolically.

As I stare in the mirror at the finished product, I'm perfectly fine with the transformation I see in front of me.

I wouldn't want to repeat some of the pain or mistakes, but they were necessary to get to this point. I want to take all that I learned and be able to share while helping others to do the same. My intent is to keep bringing awareness to important issues such as these which are often swept under the rug.

And well.....It's time!

About the Author

LISA VANALLEN

Author, Abuse Advocate and Public Speaker

We must continue to bring awareness and create a space for others to speak their truths in order to begin to heal.

This is one of my major purposes for the website www.iamlisavanallen.com.

You don't have to walk alone. Please visit the site and share your story so that others may walk with you and you may walk with them. Together we are stronger and together we will continue to SURVIVE!

Closing Remarks

I've debated in my mind for the longest time, whether or not I should write my story or how my story should be told. At the end of the day, I just felt it was long overdue. It's not about ruining the abuser or chasing fame. It's about sounding the alarm of awareness until it becomes a resounding gong that can no longer be ignored. Many people have asked "why?" or "why now?" However, have you asked yourself how many times a victim has sat across the table from their abuser or bumped into them at family functions? Have you asked how many have reported their abuse, without getting any form of justice until the abuser becomes known as a repeat offender?

It is because of issues like this, that so many have suffered and remained silent. They are silenced by the trauma, the shame as well as the mental and emotional pain. They most often fear the consequences of reporting it, which brings more shame, awkward stares, and often loss of relationships. Knowing they are not alone, gives them back some of their power and creates a safe space for them to speak their truth and start to heal. This helps create a safe space for others to do the same.

Just as the doctor goes in to surgically remove a cancerous tumor to keep the rest of the body healthy, we have to carve out the cancers that exist in our own communities. Not just the ones in the spotlight, but the ones next door, the ones we live with, that pastor or deacon in the church, the neighborhood babysitter, the family friend, the "aunt" or "uncle", the older cousin, or the teacher at school. These are just some of the faces of sexual abusers.

We can no longer sit idly by as this continues to happen.

<u>Notes to my Younger Self</u>

Lots of people use affirmations to reaffirm positivity for the betterment of their future selves. We often forget to reconcile with our past selves, especially when they have experienced any mental, emotional or physical trauma. We must reconnect with our younger selves to have a better state of emotions to connect with ourselves at those periods of our lives.

I challenge you to do the same, share your notes with me and others on Instagram: @iamlisavanallen or visit www.iamlisavanallen.com

Treat yourself like someone you've loved.
You are enough!
You are what you're looking for ......♥

Love yourself 1st!

Don't be afraid to let the wind blow through your hair. Life is never picture perfect, but your imperfections can be the very thing that perfect you. Learn to push past your flaws and mistakes to be better every day.

You are such a special creation! You may feel abandoned and unwanted because of your beginnings, but you should always remember you are valued and you are valuable for who you are in this world. You may experience the darkness in this life, but never let it dim your light or the genuine love in your heart. Approach every day with the same bright eyes you have now. Each day is a rebirth; a new chance to start fresh, change the course, plant new seeds, to grow, to empower…and most importantly to love yourself and others a little more than you did yesterday.

Pelican Gang Ent.
Publishing Company

#ITWASMEB4METOO

Made in the USA
Lexington, KY
13 March 2019